JOY

JOY

Biblical TRUTHS

— *that* —

Lift You Up

B&H
PUBLISHING GROUP

NASHVILLE, TENNESSEE

Copyright © 2018 by B&H Publishing Group
All Rights Reserved
Printed in the United States of America

978-1-5359-1789-6

Published by B&H Publishing Group
Nashville, Tennessee

Dewey Decimal Classification: 242.5
Subject Heading: DEVOTIONAL LITERATURE \
BIBLE—INSPIRATION \ MEDITATIONS \ PRAYERS

1 2 3 4 5 6 7 8 • 22 21 20 19 18

CONTENTS

CONTENTS

We live in a world that seems to be engulfed in despair. We turn on the news and can almost know there's going to be a negative take on whatever is happening in the news cycle. We get on social media, and everyone seems to have more and more frustrations in their lives instead of celebrations. Even down to our music, the most popular songs are surrounded by the notion of devastation and heartache. If someone looked at our culture from the outside, they would think that we love the negative because of our concentration on it and our lack of focus on the positive in life.

It just seems that we so easily forget about the joy in our lives. When the negative pops up, it seems to be the only thing that holds our focus. Take a teenager, for instance, she could have the most beautiful face, but put a pimple anywhere on it, and it's enough to make her shameful.

Something that takes up such a small fraction of space seems to maintain all of her focus. That's how a great deal of instances are in our lives. When we think about it, we allow the little negatives in our life to overshadow the countless positives that God provides. The solution to this problem is a simple one. We cannot allow the negative to steal our joy over the positive. We have to be willing to shift our focus.

We've all met the anxious student. Whether in a study group or in class, we all know the person that moves forward with nervousness. He'll work for hours and hours on a given assignment. Lock himself in a library for days in preparation for the upcoming test, and then the entire time he takes the test, he'll sweat. He'll pray and accept defeat upon turning in the test. This same student will make the highest score on the test. There is very little joy in the times of his success because anxiety is what rules his life. Consult Scripture on how to defeat anxiety and take hold of joy.

"Therefore I tell you: Don't worry about your life, what you will eat or what you will drink; or about your body, what you will wear. Isn't life more than food and the body more than clothing? Consider the birds of the sky: They don't sow or reap or gather into barns, yet your heavenly Father feeds them. Aren't you worth more than they? Can any of you add one moment to his life-span by worrying?"

Matthew 6:25–27

———

Humble yourselves, therefore, under the mighty hand of God, so that he may exalt you at the proper time, casting all your cares on him, because he cares about you.

1 Peter 5:6–7

"Peace I leave with you. My peace I give to you. I do not give to you as the world gives. Don't let your heart be troubled or fearful."

John 14:27

———

Don't worry about anything, but in everything, through prayer and petition with thanksgiving, present your requests to God. And the peace of God, which surpasses all understanding, will guard your hearts and minds in Christ Jesus.

Philippians 4:6–7

———

For God has not given us a spirit of fear, but one of power, love, and sound judgment.

2 Timothy 1:7

Lord, there are so many things in this world that bring me anxiety. I worry about every little thing and can barely focus on the good that You have provided in my life. Father, remind me each day of the positive in my life and guide my focus away from the negative and place it on You. Amen

Many people tend to overlook the blessings in their life. When the bad comes, the blessings are forgotten. When athletes lose, it is the only thing that keeps their focus. They don't remember the family of the team, the mentorship from a coach, the support from the fans, or the joy of winning all of their previous games. People forget the blessings when the negative comes in life. Remember the blessings that God gives each day and choose joy instead of despair.

"May the Lord *bless you and protect you; may the* Lord *make his face shine on you and be gracious to you; may the* Lord *look with favor on you and give you peace."*

Numbers 6:24–26

———

Indeed, we have all received grace upon grace from his fullness, for the law was given through Moses; grace and truth came through Jesus Christ.

John 1:16–17

———

And God is able to make every grace overflow to you, so that in every way, always having everything you need, you may excel in every good work.

2 Corinthians 9:8

Blessed is the God and Father of our Lord Jesus Christ, who has blessed us with every spiritual blessing in the heavens in Christ.

Ephesians 1:3

———

And my God will supply all your needs according to his riches in glory in Christ Jesus.

Philippians 4:19

Heavenly Father, I am sorry. I so easily forget the good that You have given me each day. I wallow in sorrow whenever there is a time of hardship. Father, allow me to recognize the blessings that You give each day. Put in me a spirit that counts each blessing, one by one. Amen

Being a nurse is a special kind of profession. They have terrible hours, work through the night, deal with sickness and stubborn patients everyday, but one thing that they will point to is how much they love their jobs. Sure, there are terrible things about the job, but the best nurses will tell you how much joy they find in their work. Most of it is because there is a joy that comes from caring for others. Look to God each day and find ways to care for others so that you may understand that joy.

*"I give you a new command: Love one another.
Just as I have loved you, you are also to love one
another. By this everyone will know that you are my
disciples, if you love one another."*
   John 13:34–35

———

*Carry one another's burdens; in this way you will
fulfill the law of Christ.*
   Galatians 6:2

Therefore, as we have opportunity, let us work for the good of all, especially for those who belong to the household of faith.

    Galatians 6:10

———

Everyone should look out not only for his own interests, but also for the interests of others.

    Philippians 2:4

Lord, God, thank You for caring for me each day. Thank You for putting people in my life that care for me in ways that I cannot even begin to describe. Lord, I know there have been opportunities to care for others and I've ignored them. Father, forgive me, and allow me to care for others the way You care for me. Amen

One of the most incredible things that we can ever do is bring comfort to others. When a young man was losing his grandmother, he held her hand, stroked her hair, and said "We all love you, so much." The elderly woman was weak, but the faintest of smiles appeared. It was a short moment, but it was so clear that the actions and words of her grandson had brought her comfort in a time of unease. When she finally passed, the twenty year old wept, but there was such a joy on his face because he had brought comfort to someone he loved one last time.

Even when I go through the darkest valley,
I fear no danger,
for you are with me;
your rod and your staff—they comfort me.
    Psalm 23:4

———

Remember your word to your servant;
you have given me hope through it.
This is my comfort in my affliction:
Your promise has given me life.
    Psalm 119:49–50

———

As a mother comforts her son, so I will comfort you,
and you will be comforted in Jerusalem.
    Isaiah 66:13

"Blessed are those who mourn, for they will be comforted."
  Matthew 5:4

———

Blessed be the God and Father of our Lord Jesus Christ, the Father of mercies and the God of all comfort. He comforts us in all our affliction, so that we may be able to comfort those who are in any kind of affliction, through the comfort we ourselves receive from God.
  2 Corinthians 1:3–4

Lord Jesus, I am so troubled. I feel like all of the walls of life are closing in on me and I don't know what to do. Father, give me peace so that I may be comforted during this time. Thank You for putting people in my life that comfort me during the tough times. Allow me to comfort others during their tough times. Amen

Every once in a while, you may just witness a show of compassion. What's interesting about these moments is that compassion is normally shown through simplicity. Helping someone change a tire, picking up something dropped by someone with full hands, even opening a door for someone can be seen as compassionate. Something you'll notice, if you take the time, is the faces of those helping others. You'll rarely see a frown on the faces of those that show compassion and help others. It's because so much joy comes from it . . . even though, more often than not, it is simple.

Yet he was compassionate;
he atoned for their iniquity
and did not destroy them.
He often turned his anger aside
and did not unleash all his wrath.
    Psalm 78:38

———

When he went ashore, he saw a large crowd and
had compassion on them, because they were like
sheep without a shepherd. Then he began to teach
them many things.
    Mark 6:34

Carry one another's burdens; in this way you will fulfill the law of Christ.

Galatians 6:2

———

And be kind and compassionate to one another, forgiving one another, just as God also forgave you in Christ.

Ephesians 4:32

Father, teach me compassion. You have provided so much of it for me. You put people in my life that love me and care for me in spite of myself. Father, put in me a heart of compassion for other people. Allow me to recognize when people need to be loved and allow me to love them the way You love me each and every day. Amen

Courtesy is the one-word definition of the Golden Rule. It is also one of the guarantees of joy. Courtesy brings joy to those that exercise it on a daily basis and also brings joy to the ones receiving it. Courtesy shows, above all, that you acknowledge a person's humanity. You take the time to do for them what you would hope someone would do for you. When we see these moments of humanity, we normally have our faith restored in it. Courtesy, though normally an easy exercise, adds massive benefits to a person's joy.

Love one another deeply as brothers and sisters.
Outdo one another in showing honor.
    Romans 12:10

———

For the whole law is fulfilled in one statement: Love
your neighbor as yourself.
    Galatians 5:14

———

No foul language should come from your mouth, but
only what is good for building up someone in need,
so that it gives grace to those who hear.
    Ephesians 4:29

Let your speech always be gracious, seasoned with salt, so that you may know how you should answer each person.

    Colossians 4:6

———

Remind them to submit to rulers and authorities, to obey, to be ready for every good work, to slander no one, to avoid fighting, and to be kind, always showing gentleness to all people.

    Titus 3:1–2

Father, I know it is easy, but I so often forget to be courteous to others. I allow myself to only focus on myself and my needs that I rarely look up to observe the needs of others. Father, allow me to recognize the needs of the people around me. Allow me to meet those needs and exercise my courtesy toward them the way You would have me. Amen

Being creative is one of the most sought after qualities in our society. One of the reasons is because a great deal of joy comes from the products of creativity. All of us can think of a favorite song, movie, book, or piece of art and take joy in just knowing that someone came up with that. People appreciate the joy that comes from creativity, but never forget from where that creativity comes. It is a gift from God.

So God created man in his own image; he created him in the image of God; he created them male and female.

Genesis 1:27

———

All things were created through him, and apart from him not one thing was created that has been created.

John 1:3

———

Do you see a person skilled in his work?
He will stand in the presence of kings.
He will not stand in the presence of the unknown.

Proverbs 22:29

*I will praise you
because I have been remarkably and wondrously
made.
Your works are wondrous,
and I know this very well.*
   Psalm 139:14

———

*For we are his workmanship, created in Christ Jesus
for good works, which God prepared ahead of time
for us to do.*
   Ephesians 2:10

Heavenly Father, thank You for the gift of creativity. Thank You for giving that gift to all of us in our own way. Lord, allow me to use that gift to glorify You. Allow me to be able to find ways to bring joy to the world by bringing You in it through the creativity You have given me. Amen

Delight is a well-known synonym of joy. People, however, often confuse delight as an equal to joy. Delight is a reaction. We take delight in good food, friendship, and good times in general, but delight does not stay in the hard times. Joy can, however, if we are willing to choose joy. How do we do that? We do this by choosing God. Choose God when life is hard. Choose God when the times seem rough. Choose God when the darkness seems to be closing in on you. Doing this will allow you to walk with joy even when the world provides no delight.

How happy is the one who does not
walk in the advice of the wicked
or stand in the pathway with sinners
or sit in the company of mockers!
Instead, his delight is in the Lord*'s instruction,*
and he meditates on it day and night.
He is like a tree planted beside flowing streams
that bears its fruit in its season
and whose leaf does not wither.
Whatever he does prospers.
    Psalm 1:1–3

———

He brought me out to a spacious place;
he rescued me because he delighted in me.
    Psalm 18:19

Take delight in the LORD,
and he will give you your heart's desires.

    Psalm 37:4

———

If your instruction had not been my delight,
I would have died in my affliction.
I will never forget your precepts,
for you have given me life through them.

    Psalm 119:92–93

———

"The LORD your God is among you, a warrior who
saves. He will rejoice over you with gladness. He
will be quiet in his love. He will delight in you with
singing."

    Zephaniah 3:17

Lord, I don't choose You everyday, and I know that I should. I know that there are times when I have chosen the ways of the world instead of You. The world has brought me delight at times, but it does not last. Guide me to choose joy in You, Father. Allow me to choose You, Lord. I know that in You is joy and everlasting delight. Amen

There have probably been times in which you were discouraged. Maybe you lost your job, a loved one, or a relationship. Whatever it is, most have walked through some level of discouragement. Something you'll notice, however, is how people handle discouragement. We all know people that seem to fall apart at the tiniest things. The smallest hiccup can bring a level of dismay that ruins their day, and yet, there are others that seem to always be able to handle their emotions in the toughest times. The reason is simple. It is a choice. They decide to live with joy. It is a choice to know that whatever may come to hinder us, it will pass; but God will always be.

The LORD is the one who will go before you. He will be with you; he will not leave you or abandon you. Do not be afraid or discouraged.

Deuteronomy 31:8

———

But he said to me, "My grace is sufficient for you, for my power is perfected in weakness."
Therefore, I will most gladly boast all the more about my weaknesses, so that Christ's power may reside in me.

2 Corinthians 12:9

In the same way the Spirit also helps us in our weakness, because we do not know what to pray for as we should, but the Spirit himself intercedes for us with unspoken groanings. And he who searches our hearts knows the mind of the Spirit, because he intercedes for the saints according to the will of God. We know that all things work together for the good of those who love God, who are called according to his purpose.

    Romans 8:26–28

———

Now may the God of hope fill you with all joy and peace as you believe so that you may overflow with hope by the power of the Holy Spirit.

    Romans 15:13

Father, I am discouraged. I feel like there is so much in the world that is against me. I feel like no matter how hard I work, I cannot seem to overcome the obstacles in my life. Father, give me the wisdom to know that with You all things are possible. That whatever is before me can be overcome with You. Remind me of this so I can take joy in that knowledge, and take joy in You. Amen

We live in a world of dissatisfaction. People seem to need more money, a bigger house, a newer car, the newest gadget. Whatever it may be, people never seem to find satisfaction. The reason is that they choose to put their joy in the temporary. Yes, there is a feeling of joy that comes from a new object, but how long does it last until we end up hating it? A person can only find true satisfaction when they put their joy in the things that are eternal.

For he has satisfied the thirsty
and filled the hungry with good things.
    Psalm 107:9

———

You open your hand
and satisfy the desire of every living thing.
    Psalm 145:16

———

The LORD will always lead you, satisfy you in a
parched land, and strengthen your bones. You will
be like a watered garden and like a spring whose
water never runs dry.
    Isaiah 58:11

"I am the bread of life," Jesus told them. "No one who comes to me will ever be hungry, and no one who believes in me will ever be thirsty again."
    John 6:35

———

Now may the God of hope fill you with all joy and peace as you believe so that you may overflow with hope by the power of the Holy Spirit.
    Romans 15:13

Lord, I never feel satisfied. It feels as if no matter what I chase after, it seems to never be enough. Father, I know that I have made my mistakes by putting my joy in the temporary. Allow me to put my joy in You, Father. Allow me to recognize daily that it is You who provides the ultimate joy. Amen

A simple word of encouragement can bring such joy to a person smothered by negativity. Sometimes a good word can be all that someone needs to be drawn out of frustration and depression and into joy. It's often that all a person needs is to know that someone cares about them. If the right person encourages them the right way, it can often start the path to finding true joy in the One that always encourages and never lets someone down.

The LORD is the one who will go before you. He will be with you; he will not leave you or abandon you. Do not be afraid or discouraged.

    Deuteronomy 31:8

———

God is our refuge and strength,
a helper who is always found
in times of trouble.

    Psalm 46:1

———

"Aren't five sparrows sold for two pennies? Yet not one of them is forgotten in God's sight. Indeed, the hairs of your head are all counted. Don't be afraid; you are worth more than many sparrows."

    Luke 12:6–7

"I have told you these things so that in me you may have peace. You will have suffering in this world. Be courageous! I have conquered the world."

    John 16:33

———

And let us watch out for one another to provoke love and good works, not neglecting to gather together, as some are in the habit of doing, but encouraging each other, and all the more as you see the day approaching.

    Hebrews 10:24–25

Lord, God, thank You for the people that encourage me when I am in a place of discouragement. Thank You for giving me the people that love and care for me enough to encourage me when I am down. Father, remind me daily to encourage those that need encouragement. Put in me a spirit that desires to lift others up, Lord. Amen

To some, faithfulness is the very definition of joy. People that walk with faithfulness often walk with joy. Why is this? It's because of the fact that people who walk with faithfulness have the understanding that whatever may come in their lives, they can move forward in knowing that God will always be there. Whenever the troubles of the world come before you, continue moving in faith that there is a God that loves you and will always be with you. It's difficult not to have joy when we have this knowledge.

*Because of the L*ORD*'s faithful love we do not perish, for his mercies never end. They are new every morning; great is your faithfulness!*
Lamentations 3:22–23

———

"His master said to him, 'Well done, good and faithful servant! You were faithful over a few things; I will put you in charge of many things. Share your master's joy.'"
Matthew 25:21

———

If we are faithless, he remains faithful, for he cannot deny himself.
2 Timothy 2:13

"*Whoever is faithful in very little is also faithful in much, and whoever is unrighteous in very little is also unrighteous in much. So if you have not been faithful with worldly wealth, who will trust you with what is genuine? And if you have not been faithful with what belongs to someone else, who will give you what is your own?*"

Luke 16:10–12

———

Let us hold on to the confession of our hope without wavering, since he who promised is faithful.

Hebrews 10:23

Lord, I have not been faithful. I have not acted like You are with me; and because of that, I have not walked with joy. Father, I know that You have never left me, even when I've walked like I've left You. Lord, remind me of Your greatness daily, and allow me to respond to that constant greatness with a faithful spirit. Amen

FAMILY

Some of the most joyous times of year are the holidays. Some people are excited about food, gifts, and vacations, but the joy that comes from these times of year is the time one gets to spend with their family. This is something that a great deal of people don't take the time to realize. When you think about that favorite dish at thanksgiving, you want it made by that special person. When you think about the gifts that come at Christmas, there are faces attached to those presents. When the thought of vacations comes to mind, there is a joy over who you get to spend that time with. Family is important; it's one of the closest things to eternity that this world has to offer, and in that, we take joy.

This is why a man leaves his father and mother and bonds with his wife, and they become one flesh.
   Genesis 2:24

———

Honor your father and your mother so that you may have a long life in the land that the LORD your God is giving you.
   Exodus 20:12

Wives, submit to your husbands as to the Lord, because the husband is the head of the wife as Christ is the head of the church. He is the Savior of the body. Now as the church submits to Christ, so also wives are to submit to their husbands in everything. Husbands, love your wives, just as Christ loved the church and gave himself for her to make her holy, cleansing her with the washing of water by the word. He did this to present the church to himself in splendor, without spot or wrinkle or anything like that, but holy and blameless. In the same way, husbands are to love their wives as their own bodies. He who loves his wife loves himself.

   Ephesians 5:22–28

———

Fathers, don't stir up anger in your children, but bring them up in the training and instruction of the Lord.

   Ephesians 6:4

Heavenly Father, thank You for family. Even when we don't have traditional families, You still provide family all the same. Father, I know that there are times that I don't appreciate the family that You have provided. Allow me to take joy in knowing that there are people that love me. Lord, allow me to love on those that may not be my family, by blood, as if they are. Amen

FEAR

Fear is the thief of joy, but fear is something that doesn't really exist when we think about it. Fear is only the anxiety over something that does not and may not ever exist. We allow fear to have so much control over our lives. Instead of living in fear of the things that do not yet exist, take joy in the Lord that has always and will always be there.

Haven't I commanded you: be strong and courageous? Do not be afraid or discouraged, for the LORD your God is with you wherever you go.
    Joshua 1:9

———

When I am afraid,
I will trust in you.
    Psalm 56:3

———

You did not receive a spirit of slavery to fall back into fear. Instead, you received the Spirit of adoption, by whom we cry out, "Abba, Father!"
    Romans 8:15

For God has not given us a spirit of fear, but one of power, love, and sound judgment.

    2 Timothy 1:7

———

Humble yourselves, therefore, under the mighty hand of God, so that he may exalt you at the proper time, casting all your cares on him, because he cares about you.

    1 Peter 5:6–7

Father, I am fearful. There are so many things in this world that I feel easily steal my joy. I know I allow these things to steal my joy. Father, protect my heart. Allow me to keep my focus on You. Instill in me an understanding that with You, I have nothing to fear. Amen

FORGIVENESS

Forgiving someone can be one of the hardest things to do. Some have hurt us on a level that we feel is impossible to forgive. Some people have put us in such a place of despair that we feel that forgiving them will let them get away with whatever they've done; but let's think about this. How do you feel when you see this person? Do you experience frustration, anger, or even hatred of this person? Forgiveness may feel as if you're letting them get away with a crime, but not forgiving will only rob you of any future joy.

"Therefore I tell you, her many sins have been forgiven; that's why she loved much. But the one who is forgiven little, loves little."
  Luke 7:47

———

Live in harmony with one another. Do not be proud; instead, associate with the humble. Do not be wise in your own estimation. Do not repay anyone evil for evil. Give careful thought to do what is honorable in everyone's eyes. If possible, as far as it depends on you, live at peace with everyone.
  Romans 12:16–18

Be kind and compassionate to one another,
forgiving one another, just as God also forgave you
in Christ.

> *Ephesians 4:32*

———

As God's chosen ones, holy and dearly loved, put on
compassion, kindness, humility, gentleness, and
patience, bearing with one another and forgiving
one another if anyone has a grievance against
another. Just as the Lord has forgiven you, so you
are also to forgive.

> *Colossians 3:12–13*

Lord Jesus, I know that I need to forgive those in my life that have wronged me. I know that it's the right thing to do. Lord, I have not forgiven these people. I have withheld forgiveness and taken hold of bitterness and anger. Lord, take these away from me. Allow me to find forgiveness for those around me and in that forgiveness, find joy. Amen

Sometimes, there's nothing better than a friend. They sometimes know us better than our own family. Friends, however, have a very special part to them. They are a choice. You choose your friends, and a lot of it has to do with the level of joy that a friend can bring you. This is not a selfish thing, when you have a good friend. They have joy when you succeed and you have joy when they succeed. When you actively love someone, joy is a by-product of that love. Be a good friend to those around you. You may just be surprised how much joy can come from that relationship.

Iron sharpens iron,
and one person sharpens another.
    Proverbs 27:17

———

Two are better than one because they have a good
reward for their efforts. For if either falls, his
companion can lift him up; but pity the one who
falls without another to lift him up.
    Ecclesiastes 4:9–10

———

Dear friends, let us love one another, because love is
from God, and everyone who loves has been born of
God and knows God.
    1 John 4:7

"No one has greater love than this: to lay down his life for his friends. You are my friends if you do what I command you. I do not call you servants anymore, because a servant doesn't know what his master is doing. I have called you friends, because I have made known to you everything I have heard from my Father."

John 15:13–15

———

Therefore encourage one another and build each other up as you are already doing.

1 Thessalonians 5:11

*Heavenly Father, thank You for friends.
Thank You for placing people in my life to
help me focus on what is important in life.
Thank You for bringing laughter and joy into
my life through the various people You have put
in it. Allow me to be a better friend to those
around me. Remind me daily that it is You from
which those friendships should be built. Amen*

A popular Christmas tradition is one called "Secret Santa." You get a name at Thanksgiving and spend the next month finding a gift for that person. You spend time getting to know the person's wants and needs and make a decision on a gift. Some families even have a rule that it has to be a gift; it can't be money or a gift card. When Christmas comes, you hopefully have given a gift that meets the needs of the person receiving the gift. There's a reason that this is a tradition. If it didn't bring a joy over giving, it would be abandoned. Consult the Scriptures on generosity and know that joy comes from it.

Good will come to the one who lends generously and conducts his business fairly.

   Psalm 112:5

———

"Give, and it will be given to you; a good measure—pressed down, shaken together, and running over—will be poured into your lap. For with the measure you use, it will be measured back to you."

   Luke 6:38

———

Each person should do as he has decided in his heart—not reluctantly or out of compulsion, since God loves a cheerful giver.

   2 Corinthians 9:7

"And if you lend to those from whom you expect to receive, what credit is that to you? Even sinners lend to sinners to be repaid in full. But love your enemies, do what is good, and lend, expecting nothing in return. Then your reward will be great, and you will be children of the Most High. For he is gracious to the ungrateful and evil."

    Luke 6:34–35

———

No one is to seek his own good, but the good of the other person.

    1 Corinthians 10:24

Lord, there are times that I struggle with generosity. I know that I hold onto what I feel is mine. This doesn't bring me joy. It makes me fearful of the days when I will lose it. Lord, put in me a heart that desires to give. Allow me to recognize the joy that comes from generosity, and remind me daily that whatever I give already belongs to you. Amen

GRACE

Grace was shown to a teen when he wrecked his grandfather's car. It was his fault. He became distracted and totaled the car in a matter of seconds. When he came to his grandfather and told him, the man simply put his hand on the boy's head and said, "It's just a car, son . . ." The boy looked to his grandfather, holding back tears, but only saw a smile. Grace was given that day simply because the grandfather had more joy over knowing his grandson was safe.

The law came along to multiply the trespass. But where sin multiplied, grace multiplied even more.
     Romans 5:20

―――――

For sin will not rule over you, because you are not under the law but under grace.
     Romans 6:14

―――――

Now if by grace, then it is not by works; otherwise grace ceases to be grace.
     Romans 11:6

But he said to me, "My grace is sufficient for you, for my power is perfected in weakness." Therefore, I will most gladly boast all the more about my weaknesses, so that Christ's power may reside in me.

    2 Corinthians 12:9

———

For you are saved by grace through faith, and this is not from yourselves; it is God's gift—not from works, so that no one can boast.

    Ephesians 2:8–9

Heavenly Father, thank You for showing me grace. I know that there are countless moments where I don't deserve it. I know that it is because of Your love for me that I have received grace. Lord, allow me to give grace to others. Allow me to have a heart of compassion and understanding when people fall. Allow me to know the joy that comes from grace. Amen

Tiffany was close to her grandmother. Many people often said she was just like her grandmother in many ways. When she passed, there was an enormous amount of grief that came over her. She had trouble finding sleep and would cry brokenly, but she never lost her sense of peace. When asked why she seemed to be calm over such a heart-wrenching situation, she would look at you and say, "She's in a better place . . . She's home . . ." She was able to take the grief that comes from loss and find joy in the knowledge of God having a place for her grandmother. Pray to God and seek after Him in the times of darkness. It will bring you joy when you least expect it.

The righteous cry out, and the LORD hears,
and rescues them from all their troubles.
The LORD is near the brokenhearted;
he saves those crushed in spirit.

    Psalm 34:17–18

———

Though the fig tree does not bud and there is no
fruit on the vines, though the olive crop fails
and the fields produce no food, though the flocks
disappear from the pen and there are no herds in
the stalls, yet I will celebrate in the LORD; I will
rejoice in the God of my salvation!

    Habakkuk 3:17–18

Then the young women will rejoice with dancing,
while young and old men rejoice together. I
will turn their mourning into joy, give them
consolation, and bring happiness out of grief.
 Jeremiah 31:13

———

"So you also have sorrow now. But I will see you
again. Your hearts will rejoice, and no one will take
away your joy from you."
 John 16:22

———

Why, my soul, are you so dejected?
Why are you in such turmoil?
Put your hope in God, for I will still praise him,
my Savior and my God.
 Psalm 42:5

Lord, I am grieving. My heart is broken. I feel lost and hopeless. Father, I know that there are times where I have been broken. I have let those moments consume me and allowed those moments to steal the joy in my life. Father, remind me to find the joy in the grief. Allow me to be able to recognize the good in the bad, the light in the darkness. Amen

Happiness is fleeting. We are happy when we reunite with friends, but they, eventually, have to go back to their lives. We're happy when we get a new car, but a time comes when it needs to be replaced. We are happy when we go on vacation, but we inevitably return to work. Happiness comes, and happiness goes, but joy . . . joy is something that lasts. It is something that moves past the temporary and into the lasting. We can't simply be happy with God simply because happiness is temporary. Take joy in the Lord, and you will find a happiness that exceeds the temporary and moves into the everlasting.

Therefore my heart is glad
and my whole being rejoices;
my body also rests securely.
   Psalm 16:9

————

Take delight in the Lord,
and he will give you your heart's desires.
   Psalm 37:4

————

A joyful heart makes a face cheerful,
but a sad heart produces a broken spirit.
   Proverbs 15:13

I know that there is nothing better for them than to rejoice and enjoy the good life.
    Ecclesiastes 3:12

————

Rejoice in the Lord always. I will say it again: Rejoice!
    Philippians 4:4

Lord, thank You for all of the happy moments in my life. Thank You for all of the things that bring me happiness. Lord, I want more. I want joy. Lord, allow me to appreciate the happiness in my life, but drive me to seek the joy found in chasing after You. Amen

Health is something to be cherished. It can be the source of great joy. The way one works on their health is what determines their level of joy. If a person works on their health, they will find joy in what their health brings them: strength, longevity, and vitality. If someone doesn't work on their health, they often find the things that come with an unhealthy lifestyle: sluggishness, sickness, and weakness. The same goes for God. Those of us that are constantly working on our relationship with Him have an easier time finding joy. Those of us that don't, normally see all the faults in the world, because it is our relationship with the world on which we work.

My flesh and my heart may fail,
but God is the strength of my heart,
my portion forever.
     Psalm 73:26

———

He heals the brokenhearted
and bandages their wounds.
     Psalm 147:3

———

Don't be wise in your own eyes;
fear the LORD and turn away from evil.
This will be healing for your body
and strengthening for your bones.
     Proverbs 3:7–8

Don't you know that your body is a temple of the Holy Spirit who is in you, whom you have from God? You are not your own, for you were bought at a price. So glorify God with your body.

    1 Corinthians 6:19–20

———

So, whether you eat or drink, or whatever you do, do everything for the glory of God.

    1 Corinthians 10:31

Father, thank You for my health. Thank You for allowing me to recognize the kind of joy that comes from a healthy lifestyle. Father, one part of my health that I need to work on is my relationship with You. Put in me a heart that seeks a relationship with You. Allow me to recognize that kind of health and joy that I'm seeking is something that only comes from You. Amen

There is a certain joy that comes from having hope. Hope is simply believing in the positive before it gets here. Whenever we find people that believe in the power of hope, we find people that also seem to hold onto joy. It all comes down to what we put our hope in.

Do you put your faith in the world that is constantly known for letting you down, or do you put your hope in God, who has never and will never fail.

But those who trust in the LORD
will renew their strength;
they will soar on wings like eagles;
they will run and not become weary,
they will walk and not faint.
    Isaiah 40:31

———

I wait for the LORD; I wait
and put my hope in his word.
    Psalm 130:5

———

Now may the God of hope fill you with all joy and
peace as you believe so that you may overflow with
hope by the power of the Holy Spirit.
    Romans 15:13

We have also obtained access through him by faith into this grace in which we stand, and we rejoice in the hope of the glory of God. And not only that, but we also rejoice in our afflictions, because we know that affliction produces endurance, endurance produces proven character, and proven character produces hope.

Romans 5:2–4

———

Let us run with endurance the race that lies before us, keeping our eyes on Jesus, the source and perfecter of our faith. For the joy that lay before him, he endured the cross, despising the shame, and sat down at the right hand of the throne of God. For consider him who endured such hostility from sinners against himself, so that you won't grow weary and give up.

Hebrews 12:1–3

Heavenly Father, thank You for showing me that You are the One who I can place my hope. I know that there are so many times that I am hopeful over the little things that don't matter or even let me down. Lord, remind me to place my hope in You. Remind me daily that it is in You that I can always place my hope. Amen

JOY

We can't exactly have a focus on joy and not mention it, can we? Where do we find joy? Where does it come from? Is it the same as just being happy, or is it something more? The fact is this. Joy comes through how we decide to look at life . . . it's dependent upon our attitude. Joy comes from what we put our faith in, where we find our hopes, our purpose. Joy is a by-product of a choice. Choose God, and find joy.

You reveal the path of life to me;
in your presence is abundant joy;
at your right hand are eternal pleasures.
    Psalm 16:11

———

This is the day the LORD has made;
let us rejoice and be glad in it.
    Psalm 118:24

But the fruit of the Spirit is love, joy, peace,
patience, kindness, goodness, faithfulness,
gentleness, and self-control. The law is not against
such things.

    Galatians 5:22–23

———

As the Father has loved me, I have also loved you.
Remain in my love. If you keep my commands
you will remain in my love, just as I have kept my
Father's commands and remain in his love. I have
told you these things so that my joy may be in you
and your joy may be complete.

    John 15:9–11

Lord, thank You. Thank You for bringing joy into my life. Lord, I need to be reminded each day that it is only through You that I can find true joy. It is only through my relationship with You that joy becomes part of my life. Thank You for loving me, Father, and allow me to respond to that love with joy each day. Amen

No one finds joy in loneliness. Even introverts will tell you that though they enjoy alone time, there is an element of interaction that they need in life. It may be hard, but we have to take a step and reach out for those around you. God did not call us to be alone. The Bible speaks extensively on family, friends, and loved ones, but also know that you are never alone. Know that God is always with you. Even when you feel like there is no one, know that there is always God, and in that take joy.

"My presence will go with you, and I will give you rest."

    Exodus 33:14

———

The LORD is the one who will go before you. He will be with you; he will not leave you or abandon you. Do not be afraid or discouraged.

    Deuteronomy 31:8

———

God provides homes for those who are deserted. He leads out the prisoners to prosperity, but the rebellious live in a scorched land.

    Psalm 68:6

*He heals the brokenhearted
and bandages their wounds.*
   Psalm 147:3

———

*Blessed be the God and Father of our Lord Jesus
Christ, the Father of mercies and the God of all
comfort. He comforts us in all our affliction, so that
we may be able to comfort those who are in any
kind of affliction, through the comfort we ourselves
receive from God.*
   2 Corinthians 1:3–4

Lord, thank You for showing us that we are never alone. Thank You for constantly being with me each and every day. Lord, I am lonely at times. I feel as if I can't seem to fit in with anyone. I feel like no matter how hard I try, there is a barrier that keeps me from connecting with others. Father, remove that barrier. Allow me to grow stronger relationships with those around me. Thank You for never leaving me, Lord. Amen

Love is one of the things that is most often tied to joy. With marriage, children, family, and friends, something very special happens. You find yourself finding joy with them even when their happiness is not your own. When they succeed, you take joy in their success. When they thrive, you take joy in knowing that they are doing well; and when they find joy, you find joy because of your love for them. Love is similar to joy in that it all depends on how you look at someone. If someone does well, and you do not find joy, do you really love them?

"But I say to you who listen: Love your enemies, do what is good to those who hate you, bless those who curse you, pray for those who mistreat you."

Luke 6:27–28

———

Love is patient, love is kind. Love does not envy, is not boastful, is not arrogant, is not rude, is not self-seeking, is not irritable, and does not keep a record of wrongs.

1 Corinthians 13:4–5

———

Above all, maintain constant love for one another, since love covers a multitude of sins.

1 Peter 4:8

God's love was revealed among us in this way: God sent his one and only Son into the world so that we might live through him.

    1 John 4:9

———

And we have come to know and to believe the love that God has for us. God is love, and the one who remains in love remains in God, and God remains in him.

    1 John 4:16

Father, thank You for loving me enough to send Your Son down to Earth. Thank You for loving me enough to save me from sin. Father, when I realize the kind of love You have for me, I can't help but be overcome with joy. Lord, remind me of this love daily so that I can constantly take joy in the love You have for me.

PEACE

To have peace is to have understanding. When tragedy strikes, you will often be able to find those that have peace. In times of dismay, you'll find a soft smile and a spirit that's excited to press forward. Peace is about finding joy in the bad moments. It's about finding the positive in the negative. Peace is not about being calm in the bad as much as it is about finding joy in a time that seems to be without it.

You will keep the mind that is dependent on you in perfect peace, for it is trusting in you.

  Isaiah 26:3

———

For I am persuaded that neither death nor life, nor angels nor rulers, nor things present nor things to come, nor powers, nor height nor depth, nor any other created thing will be able to separate us from the love of God that is in Christ Jesus our Lord.

  Romans 8:38–39

"Peace I leave with you. My peace I give to you. I do not give to you as the world gives. Don't let your heart be troubled or fearful."

John 14:27

———

And the peace of God, which surpasses all understanding, will guard your hearts and minds in Christ Jesus. Finally brothers and sisters, whatever is true, whatever is honorable, whatever is just, whatever is pure, whatever is lovely, whatever is commendable—if there is any moral excellence and if there is anything praiseworthy—dwell on these things.

Philippians 4:7–8

Lord, I have trouble finding peace. I feel like I am trapped by the negative in my life. Father, remind me that peace is simply finding the positive in the negative and keeping that as my focus. Lord, help me to focus on the positive that You have put in my life. Allow me to know that the good in life is something that points to You. Amen

When someone has purpose, you'll often find joy accompanying that purpose. When someone finds purpose in what they do, they find that joy is something that naturally flows from whatever they do. We can recognize the people that have purpose in their jobs because there is normally a joy that comes from the worker. The interesting thing is that it isn't so much the job as it is the worker's attitude toward that job. A mechanic can do the work for the paycheck and be miserable, but a different mechanic can see his job as helping people, and they will have joy because of that purpose. Simply put, recognize your purpose in what you do, and joy will come from it.

*When all has been heard, the conclusion of the
matter is this: fear God and keep his commands,
because this is for all humanity.*
    Ecclesiastes 12:13

———

*"My Father is glorified by this: that you produce
much fruit and prove to be my disciples."*
    John 15:8

———

*But I consider my life of no value to myself; my
purpose is to finish my course and the ministry I
received from the Lord Jesus, to testify to the gospel
of God's grace.*
    Acts 20:24

He has saved us and called us with a holy calling, not according to our works, but according to his own purpose and grace, which was given to us in Christ Jesus before time began.

   2 Timothy 1:9

———

Sing to him; sing praise to him; tell about all his wondrous works! Honor his holy name; let the hearts of those who seek the Lord *rejoice.*

   1 Chronicles 16:9–10

Father, allow me to find my purpose. Allow me to see what I do as more than just a job or a responsibility, but allow me to find purpose in the things that I do. Lord, if I can't find purpose in the things I do, allow for me to find the things that do give me a purpose, and remind me, Lord, that everything I do should have the purpose of glorifying You. Amen

Ask anyone that's been in a relationship and they will probably acknowledge that relationships change. In marriage, forgetting to make the bed can be seen as free-spirited, but give it a few years, and that free-spiritedness gets marked with laziness. A person's spitfire attitude will shift to argumentative in a couple of years, but a relationship built on God will show a level of joy in others people can rarely understand. Put God as the foundation of your relationships and you will find that joy will be the outcome of the daily interactions with those relationships.

Then the LORD God said, "It is not good for the man to be alone. I will make a helper corresponding to him."

Genesis 2:18

———

But if they do not have self-control, they should marry, since it is better to marry than to burn with desire.

1 Corinthians 7:9

———

Don't become partners with those who do not believe. For what partnership is there between righteousness and lawlessness? Or what fellowship does light have with darkness?

2 Corinthians 6:14

Therefore encourage one another and build each other up as you are already doing.

    1 Thessalonians 5:11

———

Above all, maintain constant love for one another, since love covers a multitude of sins.

    1 Peter 4:8

Lord, thank You for the relationships in my life. I know that there are times that we argue with one another. I know there are times I focus on the negatives in other people. Lord, allow me to constantly build my relationships off of You. Remind me to know that when a relationship is built on You, there is patience, love, understanding, accountability, and above all, joy. Amen

Stress is something that comes at almost any time. It can come with work, with relationships, even at church. Stress is like a storm; it can pop up out of nowhere, but it all comes down to how someone handles that stress. Can you find joy in the stressful moments that allow you to move forward, or do you allow the stress to overwhelm you and leave you in despair? When the storms of life pop up, hold onto God and find joy in Him.

Cast your burden on the LORD,
and he will sustain you;
he will never allow the righteous to be shaken.
    Psalm 55:22

———

Commit your activities to the LORD,
and your plans will be established.
    Proverbs 16:3

———

For I am the LORD *your God,*
who holds your right hand,
who says to you, "Do not fear,
I will help you."
    Isaiah 41:13

"Come to me, all of you who are weary and burdened, and I will give you rest. Take up my yoke and learn from me, because I am lowly and humble in heart, and you will find rest for your souls. For my yoke is easy and my burden is light."

   Matthew 11:28–30

———

I am able to do all things through him who strengthens me.

   Philippians 4:13

Father, I know that stress is temporary, but I so often don't act like it. I allow stress to defeat me. Lord, put in me a triumphant spirit that moves past the stress. Allow me to be able to push through the stressful moments with You as my guide, and allow me to find rest in You in the times that I need to rest. Amen

Joy comes from the success that people have given hard work and time. We find joy in the things on which we work. Even when we don't succeed the way we expected, there is still an element of joy found in the work that was accomplished. When we work hard for something, joy and pride are found in the things we've worked toward. Ask most silver medalists and they will tell you they would've liked to win, but being able to make it to the Olympics in the first place is something in which they found joy. Like success in this world, work on your relationship with God, and find joy in Him.

Take delight in the Lord,
and he will give you your heart's desires.
  Psalm 37:4

––––––

Commit your activities to the Lord,
and your plans will be established.
  Proverbs 16:3

"For what will it benefit someone if he gains the whole world yet loses his life? Or what will anyone give in exchange for his life? For the Son of Man is going to come with his angels in the glory of his Father, and then he will reward each according to what he has done."

    Matthew 16:26–27

———

Humble yourselves before the Lord, and he will exalt you.

    James 4:10

Lord, God, thank You for the success in my life. Thank You for walking with me in all that I've accomplished. Remind me that in my successes, it is You that gets the glory and not me. Lord, I want to find success in my relationship with You. Remind me to pray daily and dive into Your Word so that I may know You and find joy in You. Amen

It is easy to find joy when we are thankful. One young man had never owned a new car and never really ever wanted one. He always said that it got him from point A to point B and that was all he seemed to want. Even when his friends would point out something wrong with his car, he would smile and say that it got him to them without any problems. When we are thankful, our surroundings seem to be enough, and in that, we take joy.

Give thanks to the LORD for he is good;
his faithful love endures forever.
    Psalm 118:1

———

Rejoice always, pray constantly, give thanks in
everything; for this is God's will for you in Christ
Jesus.
    1 Thessalonians 5:16–18

———

Let the word of Christ dwell richly among you, in
all wisdom teaching and admonishing one another
through psalms, hymns, and spiritual songs,
singing to God with gratitude in your hearts.
    Colossians 3:16

For we know that the one who raised the Lord Jesus will also raise us with Jesus and present us with you. Indeed, everything is for your benefit so that, as grace extends through more and more people, it may cause thanksgiving to increase to the glory of God.

    2 Corinthians 4:14–15

———

Every good and perfect gift is from above, coming down from the Father of lights, who does not change like shifting shadows.

    James 1:17

Heavenly Father, I know that there are so many things in my life that I should be thankful for, and yet, they often go unnoticed. Lord, thank You for everything good in my life, and thank You for the negative that will sharpen my walk with You. Lord, remind me to be thankful each day. Point out the blessings in my life, Lord. Amen

TRUST

There are so many things that we rely on today that we didn't twenty years ago. We rely on phones to send out and gain information at a moment's notice. We rely on social media to help us stay connected. There are so many things that we put our trust in, so many aspects of life that we have to trust to function from day to day, and when these things let us down, there is a despair like none other. This is because we've placed these things as needs. When a need fails you, there is no joy. This is where God comes in . . . you see, we need God, and with Him is an everlasting joy because He can always hold our trust and never let us down.

*The person who trusts in the L*ORD*, whose*
*confidence indeed is the L*ORD*, is blessed. He will*
be like a tree planted by water: it sends its roots out
toward a stream, it doesn't fear when heat comes,
and its foliage remains green. It will not worry in a
year of drought or cease producing fruit.
　　Jeremiah 17:7–8

————

*Wait for the L*ORD*;*
be strong, and let your heart be courageous.
*Wait for the L*ORD*.*
　　Psalm 27:14

I will be with you when you pass through the waters, and when you pass through the rivers, they will not overwhelm you. You will not be scorched when you walk through the fire, and the flame will not burn you.

Isaiah 43:2

———

And my God will supply all your needs according to his riches in glory in Christ Jesus.

Philippians 4:19

———

This is the confidence we have before him: If we ask anything according to his will, he hears us.

1 John 5:14

Father, I know that I can trust You. I know that You have never and will never let me down. I'm sorry for the moments that I've acted differently. I know that You will never fail me, and yet, I will act like it will still happen. Father, put in me a trusting heart so that I may move forward with You. Allow me to see that above all else . . . it is You that deserves my trust. Amen

The wise are often marked with joy. Through experience and hardship, they've put together what really matters in this world: family, friendships, love, hard work, forgiveness, and these are just to name a few. All of these things have the potential to bring joy, but they all have an underlying quality to the success of them: God. It is through God that these elements of life find joy. Seek the wisdom of those in your life and find that the source of all joy is found in God.

Teach us to number our days carefully
so that we may develop wisdom in our hearts.
   Psalm 90:12

———

Do not be conformed to this age, but be transformed
by the renewing of your mind, so that you may
discern what is the good, pleasing, and perfect will
of God.
   Romans 12:2

Yet to those who are called, both Jews and Greeks, Christ is the power of God and the wisdom of God, because God's foolishness is wiser than human wisdom, and God's weakness is stronger than human strength.

    1 Corinthians 1:24–25

———

Now if any of you lacks wisdom, he should ask God—who gives to all generously and ungrudgingly—and it will be given to him.

    James 1:5

Father, it is through all of the seasons in life that You have given me a wisdom of understanding. Thank You for walking with me during those seasons. Thank You for showing me that it is in You that I find joy. It is through the hard times that I've realized how easy it is to find joy in You. Lord, be with me. Continue to give me wisdom so that I may find joy in You each and every day. Amen

VERSE INDEX